Dear Church

Volume I: The Beauty of the Body and the Search for Solutions

by Kai A. Pineda

1

ISBN: 978-0-578-51346-1
KAP PUBLISHING COMPANY

Printed in USA by NJC Printing St. Louis, MO

DEDICATION

To the Body of Christ whom I love. It is time for us
to stop talking about doing better, and start talking
about becoming different.

TABLE OF CONTENTS

But in fact God has placed the parts in the body, every one of them, just as he wanted them to be. If they were all one part where would the body be? As it is, there are many parts, but one body.
1 Corinthians 12:18-20 (NIV)

I say to you today, my friends, that in spite of the difficulties and frustrations of the moment, I still have a dream. - Dr. Martin Luther King, Jr.

And he said to him, "You shall love the Lord your God with all your heart and with all your soul and with all your mind. This is the greatest and first commandment. And the second is like it: You shall love your neighbor as yourself. On these two commandments depend all the Law and the Prophets." - Matthew 22:36-40 (NIV)

INTRODUCTION

A few years ago, I met a group of like-minded individuals whose heart for God beats just as mine does. We, who began as strangers, connected from around the country to learn about marketing for authors. Through this experience we forged deep relationships that would stretch us, open us up, and ultimately draw us to become the beginning of what I hope would be solutions. Prior to gathering with my new friends, God shared with me how He would be opening doors for me to meet people I would never meet otherwise. The burning in my heart and the mandate from God told me this would be a place of healing, and a doorway for reconciliation. The funny thing is when it did, I almost missed it. What has been glorious to see and remarkable to be part of is the way in which God has orchestrated it all—from direct messages on Instagram, to homework assignments in groups, or the phone calls asking if I would have the hard conversations no one really wanted to have.

At a time when our society was gripped by the headlines of young black men shot by police officers and White America seemingly unaware of their privilege, I knew we, the Body of Christ, *The Church*, had to do more, be more—love more. We'd lost sight of who we are and who our Creator is, and we went to our respective, safe corners where our preferences outweighed the Word. We silently continued to grow our ministries with a sense of diversity, or a desire for it anyway, but all the while our real lives were scarcely integrated. I had grown up as the only African-American girl in my class until the seventh grade, when I was joined by one other. Now my world lacked the diversity I had always known, and it bothered me because my heart was not divided, and I did not want my faith to appear divided either.

God, the Creator of all, could not be happy with the injustices and the separation. We were starting to *look* like the world instead of *transforming* it.

IN ONE MOMENT, YOUR ENTIRE LIFE
CAN BE TRANSFORMED

The world can be a scary place. It can feel even more frightening when we have lost our footing and no longer feel safe in the places where we should feel the safest. In both 2015 and 2018, lives were lost in mass shootings at a local ministry in Charleston, South Carolina, and in a Synagogue in Pittsburgh, Pennsylvania.

On a Wednesday night in Charleston, a weekly Bible study and prayer service was taking place at Emanuel African Methodist Episcopal Church. Members of this more than two-hundred-year-old ministry gathered as normal and welcomed a young man, a visitor. As the senior pastor taught, questions arose, and before the group members knew it, the visitor they had never seen before declared his intention. The twenty-one-year-old, self-proclaimed white supremacist said he had to kill those in attendance, and began to fire shots from the gun he had smuggled in. He reloaded five times and killed nine people, fleeing from the scene. He was later caught, never expressing any remorse.[1]

Three years later, in 2018, the killing of eleven people in a Pennsylvania synagogue was described as among the deadliest against the Jewish community in United States history. The forty-six-year-old assailant entered the Tree of Life Congregation, where members were gathered, and

---

[1] https://en.wikipedia.org/wiki/Charleston_church_shooting

began to shout anti-Semitic slurs and a phrase no one would forget, "All Jews must die!" He sent shots into the crowd, ending the lives of those who were there to celebrate their faith. In an instant, just three years apart, the lives of these two very different religious institutions were changed forever.[2]

---

[2] https://www.cbsnews.com/news/pittsburgh-shooting-today-tree-of-life-synagogue-squirrel-hill-pennsylvania-2018-10-27-live-updates/

A woman, a congregant of EAMEC, was sharing her pain with reporters over the loss of those she knew and the sheer disbelief that someone decided to threaten their right to worship God. But it did not stop there. The most pressing thing on her mind was where would they fellowship now. The building where they felt love and community was now a symbol of death, and held within its walls a reminder that at any time, without warning, this could happen again.

All over the world, places of worship formerly known as places of refuge, now had many wondering, *could we be next?* The headlines broke my heart, but the love from other denominations was the beauty I found in the midst of this hatred displayed. A Muslim man by the name of El-Messidi began a campaign to raise money on a website called LaunchGood.com. He shared the following statement in an interview with the Washington Post,

"We wish to respond to evil with good, as our faith instructs us, and send a powerful message of compassion through action...People have much more good than they have evil...People are generally good-natured and peaceful. When people get to know each other, things like this don't happen."[3]

---

3 https://www.washingtonpost.com/lifestyle/2018/10/28/respond-evil-with-good-muslim-community-raises-money-victims-synagogue-shooting/?utm_term=.3d3d65f4183a

This small act of kindness toward someone with differing beliefs did not stop Mr. El-Messidi from seeing far beyond their doctrinal divide. I saw within this display of compassion the teachings of Christ. I wondered how we, calling ourselves Christians, could foster this same love for one another and begin to unify within our own community.

POWER TO THE PEOPLE

A friend of mine and I were talking about the racial divide and tension we both have seen and felt within the Body of Christ. She, a Caucasian woman, and I, an African-American woman, discussed the obvious differences and the personal preferences that keep us separated. Her point of view and mine were closer than we might have ever realized. Her husband said it best as he realized their world (inner circle) lacked, as he said, *color*. I spoke of my desire to bring together people from all races, as my heart was to see the Church look like the Father describes us—as His bride. The big question was how would we do this, and where would we start?

We tossed several ideas around as my friends, along with my husband and I, all agreed this was not about attacking what any one ministry was or wasn't doing. This was not about looking for pastors to align with our mission and try to get them to take on a role or position they were not ready to handle. We saw it as I think all great movements start, beginning with *us*. It was time to take it to the people who were just like us, feeling just like us, and wanting to do something about it, just like we did. It would be the body and its ability to heal itself that I believed would bring lasting transformation.

ONE BODY, BUT MANY PARTS

As a young girl, I understood very early on the word *family* was not to be taken lightly. The weight of this three-syllable word created within me a sense of belonging and community I knew family was and would be important in my life. My immediate family included four of us, but my extended family on both my father and mother's sides were large and loving. Our Thanksgiving dinners, held at my great-aunt and great-uncle's home, always brought at least seventy-five of us together. I lived for the moments I was surrounded by my cousins and everyone else in my family. And anyone and everyone was welcome—so much so that one year at our annual family reunion, we realized at the end a man who shared our meals, played our games, and fit right in with the whole family, was actually a stranger.

I carried this message of never meeting a stranger into my friendships and adulthood. When people would talk about their best friends, I would say I didn't have one because my friends were my family. The same was true for those I would grow in relationship with within the Body of Christ. Our blood relations were not based on our biological DNA but our spiritual DNA. My sisters and brothers in Christ did not have to look like me, grow up like me, dress like me, or share the same race as me, to be related. Our common denominator was Christ, and because we were adopted by the same Father (God), we were indeed family.

But over time, the divide within the four walls of our denominations and the highlighting of our differences (race, age, gender), have begun to seep into the fabric of the Body and broken us apart. We forgot how much we need one another and how our differences are what make the body work properly. I might be the ear, but without me how will we hear? You might be the legs, and without you, how do we run to tell the Good News of Jesus Christ? Together we make up a Bride the Father is sending His Son Jesus back for. We have to stop fighting within our own body and start reconciling, so we can be as effective as we are called to be in the world.

No one is more important than the other. It is together, united as one, where we can make the most impact. How can we spotlight a loving God when we don't even love our neighbors as ourselves? How can we reflect the light of Christ when we are falling prey to the dimming of this world through hate and racism? How can we pray for God to heal a land when we know every Sunday, segregation still exists within our ministries? Have our preferences and comforts become more important than the building of the Kingdom?

I want you to think about how all this makes you more significant, not less. A body isn't just a single part blown up into something huge. It's all the different-but-similar parts arranged and functioning together. If Foot said, "I'm not elegant like Hand, embellished with rings; I guess I don't belong to this

body," would that make it so? If Ear said, "I'm not
beautiful like Eye, limpid and expressive; I don't
deserve a place on the head," would you want to
remove it from the body? If the body was all eye,
how could it hear? If all ear, how could it smell? As
it is, we see that God has carefully placed each part
of the body right where he wanted it.

1 Corinthians 12:14-18 (MSG)

To be created equal in America has meant
something different for each American. Our history

tells us we have not always been equal, and our current climate shows us we still have far to go. But why within the confines of Christianity have we adopted the notion that one group, one denomination, and or one race is superior than the others? Why do we act as if one is not necessary and we can get along or carry on without one another? We cannot!

The world would have us believe we do not need anyone. The best thing you can do for yourself is to adopt a *Me, Myself, and I* attitude. If you focus on yourself and make sure you are good above anyone else, then you will be successful. The truth is, this is not true at all. Think about it for a moment —how lonely would you be if you thought you were capable of doing everything by yourself, within yourself?

I am innately an introvert. I am very comfortable being by myself and with myself. However, I am very aware of the dangers awaiting anyone who does not connect with others. Because of my role as a pastor, I am with people quite often. I would have never thought I would be a pastor. Because of my love for God and obedience to Him, I accepted the call on my life and it has allowed me to meet some of the most incredible people. I, the introvert, love meeting new people and engaging and learning about others. Their culture, ways they grew up, and their faith, intrigues me. I have learned to appreciate the nuances and subtleties of the human race. It is our unique make up that makes the world truly beautiful.

THE NEED IS GREAT

But I also want you to think about how this keeps your significance from getting blown up into self-importance. For no matter how significant you are, it is only because of what you are a part of. An enormous eye or a gigantic hand wouldn't be a body, but a monster. What we have is one body with many parts, each its proper size and in its proper place. No part is important on its own. Can you imagine Eye telling Hand, "Get lost; I don't need you"? Or, Head telling Foot, "You're fired; your job has been phased out"? As a matter of fact, in practice it works the other way—the "lower" the part, the more basic, and therefore necessary. You can live without an eye, for instance, but not without a stomach. When it's a part of your own body you are concerned with, it makes no difference whether the part is visible or clothed, higher or lower. You give it dignity and honor just as it is, without comparisons. If anything, you have more concern for the lower parts than the higher. If you had to choose, wouldn't you prefer good digestion to full-bodied hair? 1 Corinthians 12:19-24 (MSG)

Years ago, I heard a song that drove me crazy. At the time of its release, every ministry's praise team or choir sang it almost weekly. Our ministry's pastor loved the song so much it became the "Altar Call" song at the close of every Sunday morning fellowship. I felt parts of the song were not directly biblical, but I understood the sentiment. The first line of the song is what I want us to concentrate on.

"I need you, You need me, we're all a part of God's body"[4]

To be clear, this need does not call for co-dependency. It draws us to focus on the importance each one of us has within the Body of Christ. Paul writes in 1 Corinthians 12 about the concern we should have for others because together, not separate, we are one. Every single one of us is

---

[4] https://www.azlyrics.com/lyrics/hezekiahwalker/
ineedyoutosurvive.html

necessary. No one is greater than another. No one has a market on God or how things should be done. No one should be made to feel less than.

Understanding we are a *body* keeps us from staying in a posture of better-than or leading with ego. We must see dignity and honor in every person we come in contact with. We have to confront our prejudices and inherited stereotypes that keep us from knowing people who are not like us culturally but serve the God we serve. We cannot ignore the things we see. We must pay close attention to see the things that are not so visible, but need to be addressed.

BRIDGING THE GAP

The way God designed our bodies is a model for understanding our lives together as a church: every part dependent on every other part, the parts we mention and the parts we don't, the parts we see and the parts we don't. If one part hurts, every other part is involved in the hurt, and in the healing. If one part flourishes, every other part enters into the exuberance.

1 Corinthians 12:25-26 (MSG)

The word that continues to keep the body from functioning properly is *division*. Webster's dictionary defines it as, *the action of separating something into parts.* Another definition says, *disagreement between two or more groups, typically producing tension or hostility.*[5]

---

[5] Merriam-Webster Dictionary, 11th ed.

Though God has called us to be separate from the world, we have brought separation into the Body of Christ. We have focused on our ministries to a point in which we are forgetting the greater work and the commission to *go*. We look at others who share the gospel as our competition rather than our co-laborers. Our effectiveness falls into question as outsiders looking in cannot understand how we can speak of a God who is love, but amongst one another love is losing.

In 1 Corinthians 12:25, the word for *division* in the Greek is *schisma*, which means *split* or *gap*. It's also where we get the word *schism*. A *schism* is defined as a formal separation of a Church into two Churches, or the secession of a group owing to doctrinal and other difference.

One of the main schisms we have with the Body is something most will not say out loud, but remains obvious. We have "Black Church" and "White Church." With a desire for multicultural ministry in the mouths of most leaders, the work to create an environment conducive for all races has not been intentional. We fall into our personal preferences led by comfort and cultural bias. We are highly exclusive and some of us don't even know it.

God shares within us through the Word of God the vital need for one another. That each of us is not only in need of the other, but it is important to the overall makeup of the Body. When I read 1

Corinthians 12:26 in *The Message*, I am convicted by these words:

> *"If one part hurts, every other part is involved in the hurt, and in the healing."*

Why is this not true in how we deal with one another? Why are we easily offended when someone points out our need for reconciliation? Why do we run away when we are challenged to consider another person's feelings? When will we sit together long enough to hear the heart of our brother and sister with a heart of compassion?

If the Bible tells us Jesus was moved by compassion, why is compassion becoming more and more absent in our society? My heart hurts when I see injustice of any kind. My spirit grieves when the brother or sister who claims they are a child of God slurs racist remarks or attacks others. I am deeply saddened by the lack of intentionality many ministries have when it comes to diversity.

But in order to love each other, we have to begin to heal in the area of *identity*. How do you love another if you don't love yourself?

For many years I dealt with extreme low self-esteem. I did not hold one natural part of my body as lovely and spoke to it with words I did not realize were damaging to my core. I could somewhat see the things outside of myself or the abilities I had and give them some credit, but when it came to the person I looked like, the body I lived in, I wanted it to be different.

I had no idea the words I hurled onto myself affected my husband. He would hear me murmur or pass a comment under my breath attacking my body and plead for me to be as kind to myself as I was to others. He wanted me to see the beauty he was not only attracted to, but the beauty God created. How could I fully love God, but hate what He created? I thought it was simple as I separated God from the equation and felt I had a right to feel the way I did as long as it did not affect others or harm another. But it did!

The person I vowed to become one with was hurting. And if he was hurting, I know God was hurting too. Here I was, created in His image, and yet I hated the reflection in the mirror. I did not see myself as His daughter. I did not see myself fearfully and wonderfully made as the scriptures said, but I was convinced I was physically less than.

And that is the point I want to make. My lack of identity in God kept me from seeing clearly.

Could it be the same for many of us? I feel that we as the Body of Christ are in a huge identity crisis. We are confused about what we should look like, and instead of fixing the apparent problem, we gloss it over with building bigger buildings, growing bigger ministries, and seeking our own selfish ambitions over the mission of Christ—to seek and save that which was lost. We compromise to be cool. We decide who is worthy of Jesus and who is not. We dress up our pain and hide behind the shadows of tradition.

Where destruction is the motive, unity is dangerous.
- Ravi Zacharias

I often wonder if the pain of our past continues to keep us from doing the necessary work to heal. Shame is a terrible beast. Our history shows us the weight shame has played within various communities of people, whether the oppressed or the oppressor. We either defend what our ancestors did or didn't do in the past, or carry forward an oppressive spirit that causes us not to see ourselves as equal, but less than. With these defense mechanisms in play, the conversations we must have in order to exist as the Bride God calls us to be hinders us from moving forward. We say we want reconciliation, but at what cost?

To say or hope there is no cost is unrealistic at best. It will cost! And it will cost *all* sides, because enough is enough. You being offended will happen. You having to allow the Word to transform you will happen. You having to see your racism, separatism, sexism, or any other -ism will happen. Us wanting to unify—it will happen, but only when we link arms and do the work.

How? This is the question we are all asking. I do not have the golden ticket for this solution, but I do have some suggestions:

1. We have to own our part. Each of us has a role to play in the whole of the Body of Christ. This is not about position or title. When Jesus was asked what the greatest commandment is, He answered, "Love the Lord thy God will all your heart, mind and all your strength, and to love your neighbor as yourself."[6] I think many of us assume the work is heavier in the second statement about our neighbors. I, on the other hand, think the second only happens when the first is done.

Our love for others is not authentic until we learn to love God fully. We recite 1 Corinthians 13 as the love chapter, and yet most of us have not adopted this self-giving, self-sacrificing love Paul describes in the verse. We choose who to love and

---

[6] Matthew 22:36-40 NIV

how to love them, and if they do not fit into our limiting boxes, we refuse to extend love. We neglect God, His Word, and most of all His children. If I have not learned to fully trust God and love myself, loving another person will be difficult. It's the same for all of us. Do you know, or even spoken to, your next door neighbor or others in your community?

My husband and I recently moved to St. Louis to plant a home fellowship. Our next-door neighbor is an older woman who lives alone. We are not the same race, age, nor do we have much in common. But upon our arrival we told her we were adopting her and whatever she needed we would assist in meeting her needs. Ms. Judith, in return, watches our house, has seeded into our outreach missions, and consistently keeps us abreast of what is happening in the community. She was hesitant at first to receive our gesture, but now, whenever she needs us, she calls.

2. See the value in others and begin to grow from a place of truth and understanding. When we decide a person's feelings are not valid because we may not share the same experience, we are in trouble. Whether or not I agree with someone, I will always validate this person's feelings because for them—founded in truth or not—they are real. If not founded in truth, then I have an opportunity through empathy and care to share with them in a way I hope leads them to the truth.

Because we are all fighting to be right, we forget we can be wrong. And it is ok to be wrong, but not to stay wrong. We each have a story and come from different walks of life. Finding the value in each other will go a long way.

3. Keep this in the forefront of our minds: *You are not my enemy*. This must be the heart we carry for one another. While there is a real enemy roaming around, seeking whom he may devour, we are killing one another because of our stubbornness, pride, and arrogance. I cannot be angry with you for every injustice I see because you have the same color skin as someone who has actually caused harm. We cannot let the racism of the past affect the way we treat each other today, or cause us to miss authentic relationships with someone who may not look like us. When we stop fighting each other, we can go after those who need healing and are seeking refuge. We cannot set the captives free if we are still captives ourselves.

4. What is God's heart concerning that?
Whatever *that* is, we cannot have a denominational, personal preference, or culture-bias view. We have to have a Kingdom view. We have to know what the Word of God says so we can lean into it and follow it completely. This is why Scripture tells us to hide God's Word in our hearts.

When asked about racial tension and the racial divide in the Body, my answer is always, *What is God's heart concerning racism—period?*

We serve a God who does not look at the color of our skin and disqualify us because of it. We serve a God who does not discriminate, we are all beautiful in his eyes. We serve a God of justice, reconciliation, redemption, grace, love, and more. His attributes and character alone are in direct opposition to hatred and bigotry of any kind.

This question is one we cannot forget to ask ourselves when we believe we are *right*. If we are to be the hands and feet of Jesus on this earth, then like Jesus, we must do what the Father says.

CHALLENGE

Join me for a moment while we do an exercise. You will need a pen and a piece of paper. First, create two columns and number them from one to ten. You may not fill in all ten slots on each side, and that's ok. Next, think about the people you spend the most time with whom you are not related to. In the first column, write their names. Now, think about the ministry you are part of and the brothers and sisters in Christ you would say you are close to. Write their names in the second column. Now the work begins.

Be honest and ask yourself, how many of these people whose names you've written down, who you have close relationships with or fellowship with weekly, are of another race?

Looking at your paper, how do you feel? If you notice you are not in relationship or fellowship with many people of another race, why do you think that is? This is in no way meant to condemn or point a finger at anyone, because to some degree, we are all a part of the divisions in our communities. Despite our preferences and what has been comfortable until now, we must move past *what has been* and into *what could be*. We can no longer talk about a unified body if we are not willing to be part of the healing and transformation. I say *we* because we all have a part to play in the reconciliation of ourselves. I cannot wait to see us become the *bride* our God is coming back for. Allowing the enemy to keep us separate is no longer an option. *We are the body and we are stronger together than we are apart!*

ABOUT THE AUTHOR

Kai A. Pineda is a pastor, teacher, speaker and worship leader whose desire is to see God's heart revealed to humanity in a way where people step into the freedom of God, and not the traditions of church. She longs for an encounter to happen with the Body of Christ where we exchange our agendas for His, pursue His love, and Prepare The Way for His return. She has committed her life to being an Ambassador for Christ and to help in leading this and the next generation into a beautiful relationship with Jesus Christ.

FOR MORE INFORMATION ABOUT DEAR CHURCH AND UPCOMING VOLUMES VISIT:

www.dearchurchbook.com

TO CONNECT WITH KAI A. PINEDA:

www.kaiapineda.com